Sherrardswood
Junior
Department

10/01

L S Dept

eggin greenback lives in this garden

the garden is at the back of a big house

eggin gets down from his mattress

now he is coming down from his tree house

there is a tin box under his tree

there are some words on the box

they are in black ink

can you read them

---

write
eggin is coming down to the garden

eggin gets up into an apple tree

he can see his playthings

he can see the garden dump

and he can see into the next garden

eggin jumps down from the tree

**write this out and write
the words in**

eggin goes up into the apple ____

he can see into the next _____

**draw eggin jumping down from
the apple tree**

5

eggin is going to go to the next garden

first he puts some things on

next he picks up the blue umbrella

now he can go

---

draw eggin with his things on

write
eggin is going to the next garden

this is the next garden

eggin can see a big greenhouse

there are some things in it

can you see them

---

draw the greenhouse

write
this _____ is in the next garden

there is a house at the end of the garden

is it a big house

next to the house there is an outhouse

can you see it

---

draw the house and the outhouse

colour them in

write

this house is at the end of the garden

there is an outhouse next to it

this is the outhouse

there is a big van in it

there are some words on the van

they are in black letters

can you read them

---

draw the van and colour it in

draw the things on it

write the words on it in black letters

write
this van is in the _____

eggin jumps into the van

he is going to play in it

he is happy

this is good fun

can he get the van going

---

write this

eggin is in the ___

can he get it going

the van is going now

can you see eggin

he is upset

the van comes out of the outhouse

can eggin stop it

---

draw eggin in the van

write

the van gets going

eggin is _ _ _ _ _

the van gets to the greenhouse

the back of the greenhouse drops down

the van goes on and on

it is going mad

it is going to bump into a big brown rock

can eggin jump out

---

draw the greenhouse

now write

the van goes bump into the greenhouse

now it is going to bump into a _ _ _ _

in the end the van gets to the rock

can you see a red spring
a yellow spring
and a green spring

there is a big crack in the rock

can you see eggin

he is under the van

---

draw this

write
eggin is _ _ _ _ _ the van

eggin creeps out from under the van

he is black and blue

he jumps up onto the rock

he can see the van

can he get it back into the outhouse

---

draw eggin up on the rock

write
eggin can see the van

the van is going to stop there

eggin creeps back to his garden

he is upset

he is going to get a good sleep